Introduction

The holiday season is the most wonderful time of year, especially when you spend it with friends, family and quilting. Whether you purchase an item with a special person in mind, prepare holiday treats in your kitchen or create something handmade, gifts that you have put your heart into will last for a lifetime and show the people you love how much you appreciate them. This book is full of projects, both large and small, that will make wonderful gifts and add personal touches to your own holiday decor.

Happy quilting!

Table of Contents

DESIGN BY WENDY SHEPPARD
QUILTED BY DARLENE SZABO OF SEW GRACEFUL QUILTING

Odd Mitten Out

Easy mitten blocks in different orientations make a fun and cheerful Christmas quilt that would be a great gift for anyone!

SKILL LEVEL
Confident Beginner

FINISHED SIZES
Quilt Size: 52½" x 61½"
Block Size: 8" x 8"
Number of Blocks: 30

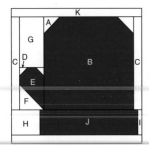

Mitten
8" x 8 Finished Block
Make 30

MATERIALS
- 10 fat eighths in assorted red, green and black prints*
- 10 fat quarters in assorted red, green and black prints*
- ⅝ yard green print*
- ⅝ yard binding fabric*
- 2½ yards white tonal
- 3⅝ yards backing
- 61" x 70" batting*
- Thread*
- Basic sewing tools and supplies

Fabrics from the Candy Cane Lane collection from Moda Fabrics; 50 wt. 100% cotton thread from Aurifil; Tuscany silk batting Hobbs used to make sample. EQ8 was used to design this quilt.

PROJECT NOTES
Read all instructions before beginning this project.

Stitch right sides together using a ¼" seam allowance unless otherwise specified.

Materials and cutting lists assume 40" of usable fabric width for yardage and 20" for fat eighths and fat quarters.

Arrows indicate directions to press seams.

WOF – width of fabric
HST – half-square triangle ◻
QST – quarter-square triangle ⊠

CUTTING
From each fat eighth cut:
- 3 (2" x 6½") J rectangles

From each fat quarter cut:
- 3 (6") B squares
- 3 (2" x 3") E rectangles

From green print cut:
- 6 (3" x WOF) strips, stitch short ends to short ends, then subcut into:
    2 (3" x 57") P strips and 2 (3" x 53") Q strips

From binding fabric cut:
- 7 (2½" x WOF) binding strips

From white tonal cut:
- 6 (2¼" x WOF) strips, stitch short ends to short ends, then subcut into:
    2 (2¼" x 53½") N strips and 2 (2¼" x 48") O strips
- 30 (2" x 3") G rectangles
- 30 (2" x 2¼") H rectangles
- 30 (2") F squares
- 6 (1½" x WOF) strips, stitch short ends to short ends, then subcut into:
    5 (1½" x 44½") M strips
- 24 (1½" x 8½") L rectangles
- 60 (1½") A squares
- 60 (1" x 8½") K rectangles
- 60 (1" x 6") C rectangles
- 30 (¾" x 2") I rectangles
- 60 (1") D squares

COMPLETING THE BLOCKS
Note: Pair the pieces cut from each fat eighth with the pieces cut from a contrasting fat quarter to make 10 piles. Work with one fabric pile at a time.

1. Refer to Sew & Flip Corners on page 6 to add two A squares to the top corners of one B square (Figure 1). Add one C rectangle to the right side. Make three.

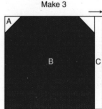

Figure 1

2. In the same way, add D squares to the top corners of one E rectangle (Figure 2). Add one F square to the bottom left corner. Make three.

Make 3

Figure 2

3. Sew one G rectangle to the top of the unit from step 2 (Figure 3). Add one C rectangle to the left side. Make three.

Make 3

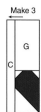

Figure 3

4. Join together one of each unit from step 1 and step 3 (Figure 4). Sew one K rectangle to the top. Make three.

Make 3

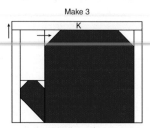

Figure 4

5. Sew together one each H, J and I rectangle and add one K rectangle to the bottom (Figure 5). Sew to the bottom of a unit from step 4 to complete one Mitten block. Make three.

Make 3

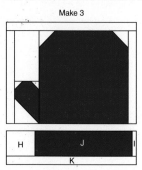

Figure 5

6. Repeat steps 1–5 to make three blocks from each fabric combination for a total of 30 blocks.

COMPLETING THE QUILT
1. Referring to the Assembly Diagram and rotating block orientation, lay out and sew together five blocks and four L rectangles into a block row. Make six block rows.
2. Sew the six block rows and five M strips together to complete the quilt center.

3. Sew N strips to opposite sides of the quilt center. Sew O strips to the top and bottom.
4. Sew P strips to opposite sides of the quilt. Sew Q strips to the top and bottom to complete the quilt top.
5. Layer, baste, quilt as desired and bind referring to Quilting Basics. The photographed quilt was quilted with an overall meandering design. ●

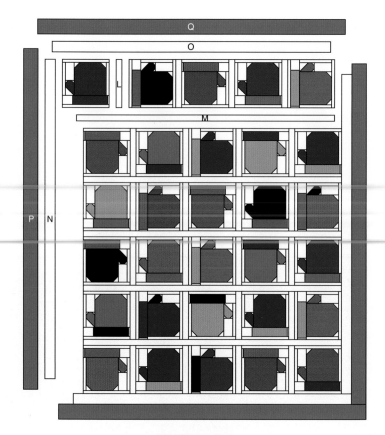

Odd Mitten Out
Assembly Diagram 52½" x 61½"

Starshine

Make this wall hanging or table topper the star of your holiday decorating! This great holiday project is easily adaptable to any color scheme or decor style.

SKILL LEVEL
Confident Beginner

FINISHED SIZES
Quilt Size: 36" x 36"
Block Size: 20" x 20" and 4" x 4"
Number of Blocks: 1 and 4

MATERIALS
- ½ yard cream print #1*
- ½ yard cream print #2*
- ¼ yard red print*
- ¼ yard green print #1*
- ½ yard green print #2*
- 1½ yards black print*
- 1¼ yards backing*
- 41" x 41" batting*
- Thread
- Basic sewing tools and supplies

Holiday Wishes from Hoffman California-International Fabrics; Warm & Natural batting from The Warm Company used to make sample.

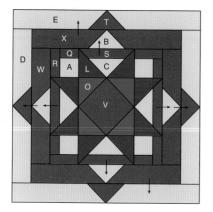

Large Star
20" x 20" Finished Block
Make 1

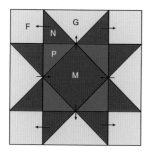

Small Star
4" x 4" Finished Block
Make 4

PROJECT NOTES

Read all instructions before beginning this project.

Stitch right sides together using a ¼" seam allowance unless otherwise specified.

Materials and cutting lists assume 40" of usable fabric width.

Arrows indicate directions to press seams.

WOF – width of fabric

HST – half-square triangle

QST – quarter-square triangle

CUTTING

From cream print #1 cut:
- 4 (2½" x 10½") E rectangles
- 4 (2½" x 8½") D rectangles
- 4 (2½" x 6½") C rectangles
- 4 (2½" x 4½") B rectangles
- 4 (2½") A squares
- 16 (1½" x 2½") G rectangles
- 16 (1½") F squares

From cream print #2 cut:
- 2 (1½" x 34½") K border strips
- 2 (1½" x 32½") J border strips
- 2 (1½" x 24½") I border strips
- 2 (1½" x 22½") H border strips

From red print cut:
- 8 (3½") L squares
- 4 (2½") M squares
- 32 (1½") N squares

From green print #1 cut:
- 4 (3½") O squares
- 16 (1½") P squares

From green print #2 cut:
- 4 (1½" x 24½") U border strips
- 4 (2½" x 4½") T rectangles
- 4 (1½" x 6½") S rectangles
- 4 (1½" x 3½") R rectangles
- 4 (1½" x 2½") Q rectangles

From black print cut:
- 2 (1½" x 36½") CC border strips
- 2 (1½" x 34½") BB border strips
- 4 (3½" x 24½") AA border strips
- 2 (1½" x 22½") Z border strips
- 2 (1½" x 20½") Y border strips
- 1 (6½") V square
- 4 (2½" x 8½") X rectangles
- 4 (2½" x 6½") W rectangles
- 4 (2½" x WOF) binding strips

COMPLETING THE BLOCKS

1. Refer to Sew & Flip Corners and use V and O squares, placing O squares on opposite corners. Add O squares to the remaining corners to make one square-in-a-square unit (Figure 1).

Square-in-a-Square Unit
Make 1

Figure 1

2. Stitch together an S rectangle and a C rectangle along long edge (Figure 2). Make four C-S units.

C-S Unit
Make 4

Figure 2

3. Lay out an A square, Q rectangle and R rectangle as shown (Figure 3). Sew A and Q together; add the R rectangle. Make four A-Q-R units.

A-Q-R Unit
Make 4

Figure 3

4. Refer to Sew & Flip Flying Geese on page 8 and use step 2 units and L squares to make four flying geese units (Figure 4).

Flying Geese Unit
Make 4

Figure 4

Here's a Tip

In order to achieve the design as shown, make sure the points of the star are stitched to the C-S units correctly! The small strip needs to end up on the outside of the finished block.

SEW & FLIP CORNERS

Use this method to add triangle corners in a quilt block.

1. Draw a diagonal line from corner to corner on the wrong side of the specified square. Place the square, right sides together, on the indicated corner of the larger piece, making sure the line is oriented in the correct direction indicated by the pattern (Figure 1).

2. Sew on the drawn line. Trim ¼" away from sewn line (Figure 2).

Figure 1   **Figure 2**

3. Open and press to reveal the corner triangle (Figure 3).

Figure 3

4. If desired, square up the finished unit to the required unfinished size. ●

5. Lay out the square-in-a-square unit, the flying geese units and the step 3 units into three rows (Figure 5). Join units together in rows; join the rows to make the star center unit.

Star Center Unit

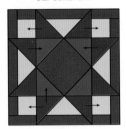

Figure 5

6. Place a W rectangle perpendicular on the right end of a B rectangle (Figure 6). Refer to Sew & Flip Corners and join the rectangles. Make two B-W units.

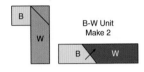

B-W Unit
Make 2

Figure 6

7. In the same manner, sew a W rectangle to the left end of each step 6 unit to make two B-W-W units (Figure 7).

B-W-W Unit
Make 2

Figure 7

8. Repeat steps 6 and 7 using B and X rectangles (Figure 8). Make two B-X-X units.

B-X-X Unit
Make 2

Figure 8

SEW & FLIP FLYING GEESE

With this method, squares are sewn onto opposite ends of a rectangle. The rectangle will be the center of the flying geese unit and the squares will become the "wings." After sewing in place, the squares are trimmed and flipped open to create the unit. The bias edges aren't exposed until after sewing so there is no concern about stretch and distortion.

Cutting
Add ½" to the desired finished height and width of the flying geese unit and cut a rectangle that size.

Cut two squares the same size as the height of the cut rectangle.

For example, to make one 2" x 4" finished flying geese unit, cut a 2½" x 4½" rectangle and two 2½" squares (Photo D).

Photo D

Assembly
1. Draw a diagonal line from corner to corner on the wrong side of each small square.

Place a square, right sides together, on one end of the rectangle. Sew just outside the drawn line (Photo E).

Photo E

2. Using a rotary cutter, trim ¼" away from sewn line.

Open and press to reveal the corner triangle or wing (Photo F).

Photo F

3. Place the second square, right sides together, on the opposite end of the rectangle. This square will slightly overlap the previous piece.

Sew just outside the drawn line and trim ¼" away from sewn line as before.

Open and press to complete the flying geese unit (Photo G).

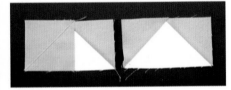

Photo G

4. If desired, square up the finished unit to the required unfinished size. ●

9. Repeat steps 6 and 7 using D, E and T rectangles to make two each of D-D-T units and E-E-T units (Figure 9).

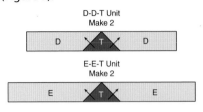

Figure 9

10. Refer to the Large Star block diagram and arrange units from steps 7–9 around the star center unit. Working from the center out, sew the units to the star center unit to complete the Large Star block.

11. Refer to Sew & Flip Corners and use M and P squares, placing P squares on opposite corners. Repeat on the remaining corners to make four M-P square-in-a-square units (Figure 10).

Figure 10

12. Refer to Sew & Flip Flying Geese and use G rectangles and N squares to make 16 G-N flying geese units (Figure 11).

Figure 11

13. Refer to the Small Star block diagram and arrange four F squares, one M-P square-in-a-square unit and four G-N flying geese units into three rows. Sew pieces and units together in rows; join the rows to complete one Small Star block. Make four.

COMPLETING THE QUILT

1. Sew one U border strip to an AA border strip along the long edge (Figure 12). Make four U-AA border strips.

Figure 12

2. Referring to the Assembly Diagram, stitch the Y border strips to opposite sides of the Large Star block; press. Stitch the Z border strips to the top and bottom; press.

3. In the same manner, sew H and I border strips to the quilt center.

4. Stitch one U-AA border strip to each side with the U strip touching the quilt center; press.

5. Stitch one Small Star block to each end of the remaining U-AA border strips. Stitch border strips to the top and bottom with the U strips touching the quilt center; press.

6. Stitch the J border strips to opposite sides of the quilt center; press. Stitch the K border strips to the top and bottom; press.

7. In the same manner, stitch the BB and CC border strips to the quilt center to complete the quilt top; press.

8. Layer, baste, quilt as desired and bind referring to Quilting Basics. The photographed sample was quilted with a loopy meander. ●

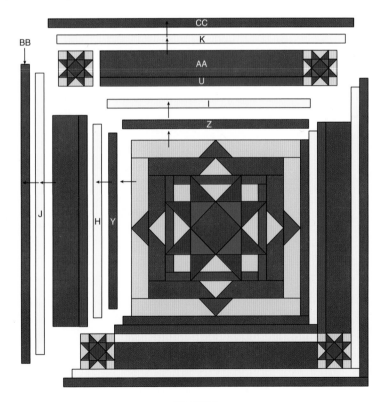

Starshine
Assembly Diagram 36" x 36"

Ornaments on the Tree

Surround your Christmas tree with colorful ornaments just waiting to be hung.

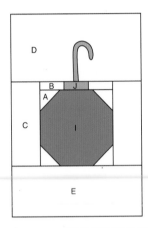

Ornament A
8" x 12" Finished Block
Make 8

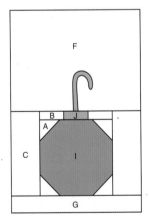

Ornament B
8" x 12" Finished Block
Make 4

SKILL LEVEL
Confident Beginner

FINISHED SIZES
Quilt/Tree Skirt Size: 48" x 48"
Block Size: 8" x 12"
Number of Blocks: 12

MATERIALS
- 2 charm packs or 72 (5") squares of assorted holiday prints*
- 1 yard white-on-white print*
- 1 yard light gray print (if not making quilt into tree skirt, only ½ yard needed)*
- ⅛ yard paper-backed fusible web
- 3⅛ yards backing*
- 54" x 54" batting*
- Thread
- Basic sewing tools and supplies

Snowkissed by Sweetwater for Moda Fabrics; Warm 100 batting from The Warm Company used to make sample.

PROJECT NOTES
Read all instructions before beginning this project.

Stitch right sides together using a ¼" seam allowance unless otherwise specified.

Materials and cutting lists assume 40" of usable fabric width.

Arrows indicate directions to press seams.

WOF – width of fabric
HST – half-square triangle ◹
QST – quarter-square triangle ⊠

CUTTING
Before cutting, set aside your 12 favorite 5" squares from the assorted prints as the I squares for ornament blocks.

From remaining assorted 5" squares cut:
- 60 (4½") H squares

From white-on-white print cut:
- 4 (6½" x 8½") F rectangles
- 8 (4½" x 8½") D rectangles
- 8 (3½" x 8½") E rectangles
- 24 (2¼" x 5½") C rectangles
- 4 (1½" x 8½") G rectangles
- 48 (1¾" x 1¾") A squares
- 24 (1" x 2") B rectangles

From light gray print cut:
- Enough 2½"-wide bias strips to yield 280" of bias binding**
- 12 (1" x 2") J rectangles

Reserve the remaining fabric for fusible appliqué.

**If not cutting the completed quilt to make a tree skirt, cut 5 (2½" x WOF) binding strips instead.*

COMPLETING THE BLOCKS

1. Referring to Sew & Flip Corners on page 6, add A squares as shown to all four corners of the reserved I squares to make 12 A-I units (Figure 1).

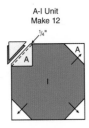

A-I Unit
Make 12

Figure 1

2. Sew B rectangles to opposite short ends of a J rectangle to make a B-J unit (Figure 2). Make 12.

B-J Unit
Make 12

Figure 2

3. Referring to Figure 3 and the Ornament A block diagram, arrange an A-I unit (noting any directional print orientation), a B-J unit, two C rectangles and one each D and E rectangles as shown. Sew B-J to the top of A-I, then add C rectangles to the sides, the D rectangle to the top and the E rectangle to the bottom to complete an Ornament A block. Make eight.

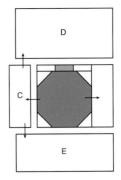

Figure 3

4. Referring to the Ornament B block diagram, repeat step 3, replacing the D and E rectangles with F and G, respectively, to make four Ornament B blocks.

5. Referring to Raw-Edge Fusible Appliqué on page 47, use the hook appliqué pattern to make 12 hooks from remaining light gray print and fusible web. Fuse and appliqué as desired to the top of each ornament in the blocks.

6. Arrange 36 H squares in six rows of six squares each (Figure 4). Sew squares into rows and sew rows together to complete a center unit, 24½" square.

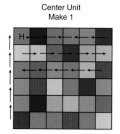

Center Unit
Make 1

Figure 4

7. Arrange six H squares as shown (Figure 5). Sew squares into rows and sew rows together, adding the sixth H square at the top to complete a corner unit. Make four.

Corner Unit
Make 4

Figure 5

COMPLETING THE QUILT/ TREE SKIRT

1. Referring to the Assembly Diagram, arrange the corner units, Ornament A and B blocks and center unit in three rows as shown.

2. Join the blocks and units into rows. Join the rows together to complete the quilt top.

3. Layer, baste and quilt as desired referring to Quilting Basics. Trim the

corner units at a 45-degree angle ¼" from the seam intersections (Figure 6).

Trim

Figure 6

4. If making a tree skirt from the completed quilt top, mark a 6"-diameter circle in the center of the quilt. Cut from the middle of one corner unit to the center of the quilt, then cut on the line to make the circular opening for the tree trunk.

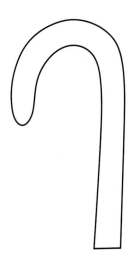

Figure 7

5. Bind referring to Quilting Basics, using bias binding for a tree skirt or straight-grain binding for a quilt. ●

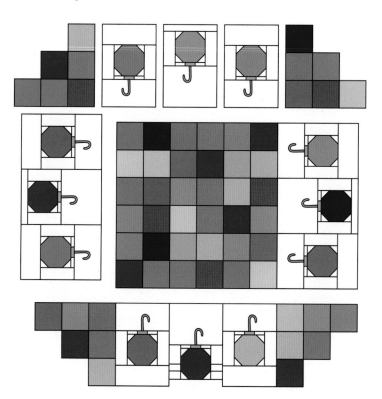

Ornaments on the Tree

Ornaments on the Tree
Hook
Cut as per instructions

DESIGN BY CASSIE HARMS
QUILTED BY TERIANN HARMS

On Christmas Day

This jolly quilt is all wrapped up and ready for Christmas morning!

SKILL LEVEL
Confident Beginner

FINISHED SIZES
Quilt Size: 40½" x 40½"
Block Size: 12" x 12"
Number of Blocks: 4

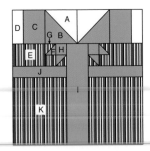

Present
12" x 12" Finished Block
Make 4

MATERIALS
- ⅞ yard white*
- ⅝ yard red and gold dot*
- ⅜ yard green and gold dot*
- ⅓ yard red and gold stripe*
- ⅓ yard green and gold stripe*
- ⅞ yard green print*
- 1⅞ yards backing*
- 48" x 48" batting*
- Thread
- Basic sewing tools and supplies

Holiday Sweets from Hoffman California-International Fabrics; Heirloom 80/20 Batting from Hobbs Bonded Fibers used to make sample. EQ8 was used to design this quilt.

PROJECT NOTES
Read all instructions before beginning this project.

Stitch right sides together using a ¼" seam allowance unless otherwise specified.

Materials and cutting lists assume 40" of usable fabric width.

Arrows indicate directions to press seams.

WOF – width of fabric

HST – half-square triangle

QST – quarter-square triangle

Here's a Tip
Be mindful of the directional print when cutting stripes or one-way designs.

CUTTING
From white cut:
- 12 (2" x 12½") L rectangles
- 4 (4") A squares
- 8 (1½" x 3½") D rectangles
- 4 (2" x WOF) M/N strips, stitch short ends to short ends, then subcut into:
  2 (2" x 29") M and
  2 (2" x 32") N border strips

From red and gold dot cut:
- 2 (4") B squares
- 2 (2½" x 9½") I rectangles
- 4 (2½" x 3½") C rectangles
- 8 (2") F squares
- 4 (1½" x 5½") J rectangles
- 4 (1½") H squares

- 4 (2¼" x WOF) O/P strips, stitch short ends to short ends, then subcut into:
  2 (2¼"x 32") O and
  2 (2¼" x 35½") P border strips

From green and gold dot cut:
- 2 (4") B squares
- 2 (2½" x 9½") I rectangles
- 4 (2½" x 3½") C rectangles
- 9 (2") F squares
- 4 (1½" x 5½") J rectangles
- 4 (1½") H squares

From red and gold stripe cut:
- 4 (5½" x 6½") K rectangles
- 4 (2½" x 3½") E rectangles
- 4 (2") G squares
- 4 (1½") H squares

From green and gold stripe cut:
- 4 (5½" x 6½") K rectangles
- 4 (2½" x 3½") E rectangles
- 4 (2") G squares
- 4 (1½") H squares

From green print cut:
- 4 (3¼" x WOF) Q/R strips, stitch short ends to short ends, then subcut into:
  2 (3¼" x 35½") Q and
  2 (3¼" x 40½") R border strips
- 4 (2½" x WOF) binding strips

COMPLETING THE BLOCKS
1. Refer to Half-Square Triangles on page 17 and use A and B squares to make four green A-B HST units and four red A-B HST units (Figure 1). Trim HST units to 3½" square.

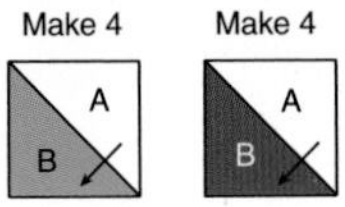

Figure 1

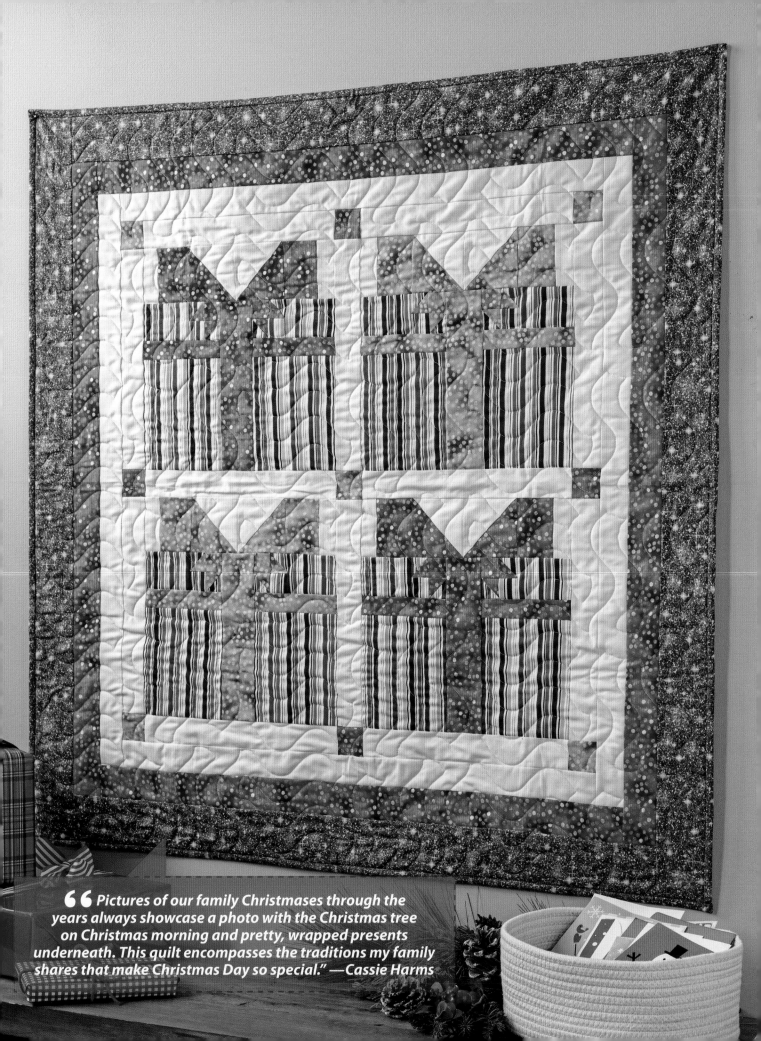

" *Pictures of our family Christmases through the years always showcase a photo with the Christmas tree on Christmas morning and pretty, wrapped presents underneath. This quilt encompasses the traditions my family shares that make Christmas Day so special."* —Cassie Harms

2. Stitch two matching A-B HST units together (Figure 2). Make four total.

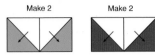

Figure 2

3. Stitch together one D rectangle and one C rectangle (Figure 3). Make eight total.

Figure 3

4. Stitch two matching step 3 units to each step 2 unit (Figure 4). Make four total.

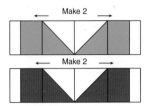

Figure 4

5. Refer to Half-Square Triangles and use green F squares and red stripe G squares to make eight F-G HST units (Figure 5). Repeat to make eight red F and green stripe G HST units. Trim HST units to 1½" square.

Figure 5

6. Arrange two matching step 5 HST units and one each matching fabric H square (Figure 6). Stitch HSTs and squares together in rows; join the rows to make four four-patch units in each color combination.

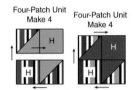

Figure 6

7. Paying attention to orientation, stitch two red stripe four-patch units to matching E rectangles (Figure 7). Stitch two mirror-image units. Repeat using green stripe four-patch units and matching E rectangles.

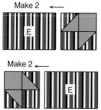

Figure 7

8. Refer to the Present block diagram and arrange one step 4 unit, one step 7 unit and matching mirror-image unit, one I rectangle and two each J and K rectangles. Stitch step 7 units, J and K rectangles together in vertical rows; sew vertical rows to opposite sides of the I rectangle and sew to the step 4 unit to complete one block. Make four.

COMPLETING THE QUILT

1. Refer to the Assembly Diagram and arrange remaining F squares, L strips and blocks in rows. Stitch together in rows; join the rows to complete the quilt center.

2. Stitch the borders to the quilt center in alphabetical order.

3. Layer, baste, quilt as desired and bind referring to Quilting Basics. The photographed quilt was quilted with a wavy line design. ●

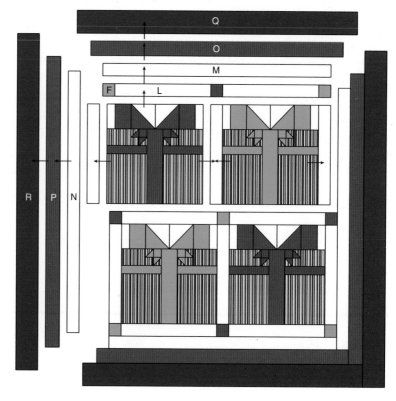

On Christmas Day
Assembly Diagram 40½" x 40½"

HALF-SQUARE TRIANGLES

Half-square triangles (HSTs) are a basic unit of quilting used in many blocks or on their own. This construction method will yield two HSTs.

1. Refer to the pattern for size to cut squares. The standard formula is to add ⅞" to the finished size of the square. Cut two squares from different colors this size. For example, for a 3" finished HST unit, cut 3⅞" squares.

2. Draw a diagonal line from corner to corner on the wrong side of the lightest color square. Layer the squares right sides together. Stitch ¼" on either side of the drawn line (Figure A).

Figure A

3. Cut the squares apart on the drawn line, leaving a ¼" seam allowance and making two HST units referring to Figure B.

Figure B

4. Open the HST units and press seam allowances toward the darker fabric making two HST units (Figure C). ●

Figure C

DESIGN BY NANCY SCOTT
QUILTED BY MASTERPIECE QUILTING

Checkerboard Stars

Oversize 16" star blocks create secondary patterns thanks to the sashing and cornerstones on this quilt. It's perfect for snuggling on the couch, to dress up a guest bed or to wrap up kiddos in the backseat while driving around looking at Christmas lights.

SKILL LEVEL

Confident Beginner

FINISHED SIZES

Quilt Size: 69" x 69"

Block Size: 16" x 16"

Number of Blocks: 9

MATERIALS

- 2¾ yards light star print
- 2 yards dark green
- 1 yard dark red
- ½ yard red print
- ¾ yard stripe
- 4½ yards of 40"-wide backing fabric*
- 75" x 75" batting*
- Thread
- Basic sewing tools and supplies

Noel by Edyta Sitar for Andover Fabrics; Warm 80/20 batting from The Warm Company used to make sample. EQ6 was used to design this quilt.

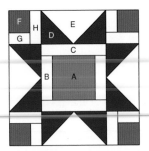

Checkerboard Star
16" x 16" Finished Block
Make 9

PROJECT NOTES

Read all instructions before beginning this project.

Stitch right sides together using a ¼" seam allowance unless otherwise specified.

Materials and cutting lists assume 40" of usable fabric width for yardage.

Arrows indicate directions to press seams.

WOF – width of fabric

HST – half-square triangle ◻

QST – quarter-square triangle ⊠

CUTTING

From light star print cut:

- 2 (16½" x WOF) strips, then subcut into:

    24 (3" x 16½") I sashing strips

- 9 (9¼") squares, then cut twice diagonally ⊠ to make 36 E triangles
- 18 (1⅞" x 8½") C rectangles
- 18 (1⅞" x 5⅞") B rectangles
- 36 (1⅞" x 4½") H rectangles
- 36 (1⅞" x 3⅛") G rectangles

From dark green cut:

- 5 (4⅞" x WOF) strips, then subcut into:

    36 (4⅞") squares, then cut each square once diagonally ◻ to make 72 D triangles

- 6 (6½" x WOF) strips, then seam on short ends to make one long strip and subcut into:

    4 (6½" x 56½") K border strips

From dark red cut:

- 1 (6½" x WOF) strip, then subcut into:

    4 (6½") L squares

- 3 (3⅛" x WOF) strips, then subcut into:

    36 (3⅛") F squares

- 2 (3" x WOF) strips, then subcut into:

    16 (3") J squares

From red print cut:
- 2 (5⅞" x WOF) strips, then subcut into:
  9 (5⅞") A squares

From stripe cut:
- 8 (2½" x WOF) binding strips

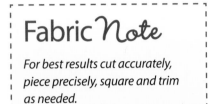

Fabric Note

For best results cut accurately, piece precisely, square and trim as needed.

COMPLETING THE BLOCKS

1. Sew B strips to opposite sides of an A square (Figure 1a); Sew C strips to the top and bottom (Figure 1b) to complete the block center (Figure 1c). Make nine.

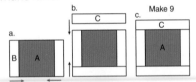

Figure 1

2. Sew two D triangles on opposite short sides of an E triangle (Figure 2a) to make a flying geese unit (Figure 2b). Make 36.

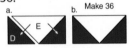

Figure 2

3. Sew a G rectangle on to the bottom side of an F square (Figure 3a). Sew an H rectangle to the right side (Figure 3b) to make a corner unit (Figure 3c). Make 36.

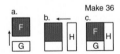

Figure 3

4. Arrange one block center from step 1, four flying geese units from step 2 and four corner units from step 3 into three rows (Figure 4). Make sure the corner units are oriented correctly. Join into rows and sew rows together to complete one block. Make nine.

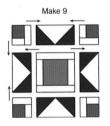

Figure 4

COMPLETING THE QUILT

Refer to the Assembly Diagram when completing the quilt.

1. Alternately sew four I sashing strips and three blocks to make a block row. Repeat to make three block rows.

2. Alternately sew four J cornerstones and three I sashing strips to make a sashing row. Repeat to make four sashing rows.

3. Alternately join sashing and block rows to complete the quilt top center.

4. Sew K strips to opposite sides of the quilt center.

5. Sew L squares to opposite ends of the remaining two K strips to make a pieced border. Make two.

6. Sew the pieced K-L borders to the top and bottom of the quilt center to complete the quilt top.

7. Layer, baste, quilt and bind referring to Quilting Basics. The photographed quilt was quilted in a large stipple pattern. ●

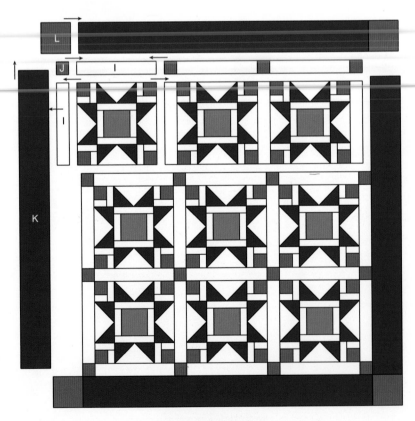

Checkerboard Stars
Assembly Diagram 69" x 69"

DESIGNED BY NANCY SCOTT
QUILTED BY MASTERPIECE QUILTING

Very Merry

Table runners are a great way to dress up a table. This one works up quickly and can be colored for any time of year.

SKILL LEVEL
Confident Beginner

FINISHED SIZES
Quilt Size: 56" x 20"
Block Size: 16" x 16"
Number of Blocks: 3

MATERIALS
- 1¼ yards cream tonal
- ⅔ yard green tonal
- 1 fat quarter each red tonal and gold tonal
- 1¾ yards backing fabric
- 26" x 62" batting*
- Tri-Recs ruler (optional)
- Thread
- Basic sewing tools and supplies

Warm 80/20 batting from The Warm Company used to make sample. EQ6 was used to design this quilt.

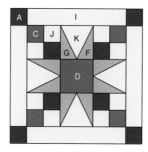

Block 1
16" x 16" Finished Block
Make 2

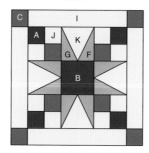

Block 2
16" x 16" Finished Block
Make 1

PROJECT NOTES
Read all instructions before beginning this project.

Stitch right sides together using a ¼" seam allowance unless otherwise specified.

Materials and cutting lists assume 40" of usable fabric width for yardage and 20" for fat quarters.

Arrows indicate directions to press seams.

WOF – width of fabric
HST – half-square triangle
QST – quarter-square triangle

Here's a Tip
Have a great time mixing and matching colors to make this runner for any season or decor.

CUTTING

From cream tonal cut:
- 10 (2½" x 16½") L rectangles
- 12 (2½" x 12½") I rectangles
- 12 (4¾") K squares**
- 24 (2½") J squares

From gold tonal cut:
- 12 (2⅝" x 5¼") F/G rectangles**
- 8 (2½") H squares

From green tonal cut:
- 4 (2½" x WOF) binding strips
- 2 (4½") D squares
- 16 (2½") C squares

From red tonal cut:
- 1 (4½") B square
- 20 (2½") A squares

**If using Tri-Recs rulers, follow ruler instructions for 4" finished (4½" cut size) units to cut 12 K center triangles from cream and 12 and 12 reversed F/G side triangles from gold.

COMPLETING THE BLOCKS

Note: *If you used the Tri-Recs rulers to precut F, G and K triangles, skip ahead to step 3.*

1. Cut six F/G rectangles diagonally from the bottom left corner to the top right corner as shown to yield 12 F triangles (Figure 1). Cut the remaining rectangles diagonally in the opposite direction to yield 12 G triangles.

Cut 6 rectangles
in each direction

Figure 1

2. Fold each K square in half and finger-press a crease at the center on one side. Cut from opposite corners to the center as shown to yield 12 K triangles (Figure 2).

Cut 12

Center

Figure 2

3. Sew an F and a G triangle on opposite sides of a K triangle to make an F-G-K unit; press (Figure 3). Repeat to make a total of 12 F-G-K units. If needed, trim to square up to 4½" x 4½".

F-G-K Unit
Make 12

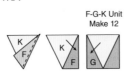

Figure 3

4. Arrange and sew two J and one each A and C squares together to make an A-C-J unit (Figure 4). Repeat to make a total of 12 A-C-J units.

A-C-J Unit
Make 12

Figure 4

5. Referring to the Block 1 diagram, arrange four each A-C-J and F-G-K units and one D square into three rows of three. Join into rows, then join rows together to make a block center; press.

6. Sew I rectangles on opposite sides of the block center; press toward I.

7. Sew A squares on opposite ends of an I rectangle to make an A-I unit; press toward I. Repeat to make two.

8. Sew A-I units to the top and bottom of the unit from step 2 to complete one Block 1.

9. Repeat steps 5–8 to make a second Block 1.

10. Referring to the Block 2 diagram, arrange four each A-C-J and F-G-K units and one B square into three rows of three. Join into rows, then join rows together to make a block center; press.

11. Repeat steps 6–8, replacing A squares with C squares, to complete one Block 2.

COMPLETING THE RUNNER

1. Alternately arrange four L rectangles with Blocks 1 and 2 and sew together to make the center row.

2. Alternately arrange four H squares and three L rectangles to make a border row. Sew together. Repeat to make a second border row.

3. Sew border rows to the top and bottom of the center row to complete the runner; press.

4. Layer, baste, quilt as desired and bind referring to Quilting Basics. The star points were quilted with straight lines ¼" from the seam lines and the background was quilted with a meander in the photographed quilt. ●

Very Merry
Assembly Diagram 56" x 20"

DESIGN BY WENDY SHEPPARD
QUILTED BY DARLENE SZABO OF SEW GRACEFUL QUILTING

Jingle Bells

Simple and easy bell blocks make a fun Christmas tree when creatively stacked!

SKILL LEVEL
Confident Beginner

FINISHED SIZES
Quilt Size: 74" x 80"
Block Size: 9" x 9"
Number of Blocks: 22

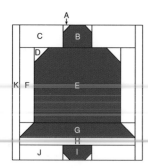

Bell
9" x 9" Finished Block
Make 21

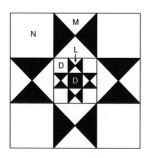

Star
9" x 9" Finished Block
Make 1

MATERIALS
- 22 (10") squares (from Layer Cake or assorted)*
- ¾ yard binding fabric*
- 1⅛ yards white print*
- 4¾ yards white tonal*
- 5 yards backing
- 82" x 88" batting*
- Thread*
- Basic sewing tools and supplies

Fabrics from the Joyful, Joyful collection by Stacy Iest Hsu for Moda Fabrics; Mako 50wt thread from Aurifil; Tuscany silk batting from Hobbs Bonded Fibers used to make sample. EQ8 was used to design this quilt.

PROJECT NOTES
Read all instructions before beginning this project.

Stitch right sides together using a ¼" seam allowance unless otherwise specified.

Materials and cutting lists assume 40" of usable fabric width for yardage.

Arrows indicate directions to press seams.

WOF – width of fabric
HST – half-square triangle �%
QST – quarter-square triangle ⊠

CUTTING
**From one 10" square
(for Star block) cut:**

- 2 (4½") M squares
- 2 (2½") L squares
- 1 (1½") D square

**From each remaining
10" square cut:**

- 1 (5½" x 6½") E rectangle
- 1 (2" x 2½") B rectangle
- 1 (1½" x 8½") G rectangle
- 1 (1½" x 2½") I rectangle

From binding fabric cut:
- 8 (2½" x WOF) binding strips

From white print cut:
- 8 (4" x WOF) strips, stitch short ends to short ends, then subcut into:
  2 (4" x 74½") Y strips and 2 (4" x 73½") X strips

From white tonal cut:
- 7 (2½" x WOF) strips, stitch short ends to short ends, then subcut into:
  2 (2½" x 69½") V strips and 2 (2½" x 67½") W strips
- 11 (1½" x WOF) strips, stitch short ends to short ends, then subcut into:
  6 (1½" x 63½") U strips
- 4 (9½" x 27½") O rectangles
- 2 (9½" x 23") P rectangles
- 2 (9½" x 18½") Q rectangles
- 2 (9½" x 14") R rectangles
- 2 (9½") S squares
- 2 (5" x 9½") T rectangles
- 2 (4½") M squares
- 4 (3½") N squares
- 2 (2½") L squares
- 42 (2" x 3½") C rectangles
- 42 (1½" x 5½") F rectangles
- 42 (1½" x 3½") J rectangles
- 88 (1½") D squares
- 42 (1" x 9½") K rectangles
- 21 (1" x 8½") H rectangles
- 84 (1") A squares

COMPLETING THE BELL BLOCKS

1. Refer to Sew & Flip Corners on page 6 to add two A squares to the top corners of one B rectangle (Figure 1). Sew C rectangles to opposite sides to make one A-B-C unit. Make 21.

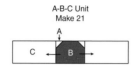

A-B-C Unit
Make 21

Figure 1

2. In the same way, add D squares to the top corners of one E rectangle, noting orientation (Figure 2). Sew F rectangles to opposite sides to make one D-E-F unit. Make 21.

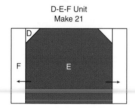

D-E-F Unit
Make 21

Figure 2

3. In the same way, add D squares to one G rectangle to make one D-G unit (Figure 3). Make 21.

D-G Unit
Make 21

Figure 3

4. In the same way, add two A squares to the bottom corners of one I rectangle (Figure 4). Sew J rectangles to opposite sides and one H rectangle to the top to make one H-I-J unit. Make 21.

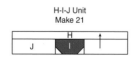

H-I-J Unit
Make 21

Figure 4

5. Sew one of each unit from steps 1–4 together and add K rectangles to opposite sides to complete a Bell block (Figure 5). Make 21.

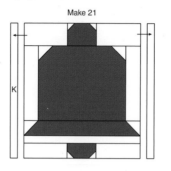

Make 21

Figure 5

COMPLETING THE STAR BLOCK

1. Refer to Quarter-Square Triangles on page 27 and use one each white and print L square to make two L units (Figure 6). Make four matching L units. In the same way, make four matching M units.

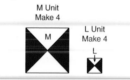

M Unit
Make 4

L Unit
Make 4

Figure 6

2. Lay out four white D squares, one print D square and four L units into three rows of three (Figure 7). Sew into rows and join the rows to make the star center unit.

Figure 7

3. Lay out four N squares, four M units and the star center unit into three rows of three. Sew into rows and join the rows to make the Star block.

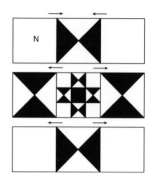

Figure 8

COMPLETING THE QUILT

1. Referring to the Assembly Diagram, lay out the Bell and Star blocks into seven rows. Lay out the indicated O, P, Q, R, S or T pieces to opposite sides of each row. Sew the pieces and blocks into rows.

2. Sew the block rows together, alternating with six U strips, to complete the quilt center.

3. Sew V strips to opposite sides of the quilt center. Sew W strips to the top and bottom.

4. Sew X strips to opposite sides of the quilt. Sew Y strips to the top and bottom to complete the quilt top.

5. Layer, baste, quilt as desired and bind referring to Quilting Basics. The photographed quilt was quilted with a freehand swirl design. ●

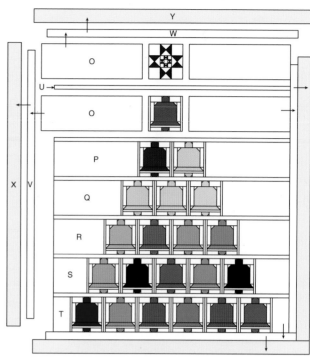

Jingle Bells
Assembly Diagram 74" x 80"

QUARTER-SQUARE TRIANGLES

Quarter-square triangles (QSTs) are a basic unit of quilting used in many blocks or on their own. This construction method will yield two QST units.

1. Refer to the pattern for size to cut squares. The standard formula is to add 1¼" to the finished size of the square. Cut two squares from different colors this size. For example, for a 3" finished QST unit, cut 4¼" squares.

2. Draw a diagonal line from corner to corner on the wrong side of the lightest color square. Layer the squares right sides together. Stitch ¼" on either side of the drawn line. Cut apart on the drawn line to yield two half-square triangle (HST) units. Open and press toward the darker fabric (Figure A).

Figure A

3. Draw a diagonal line from corner to corner on the wrong side of one HST unit perpendicular to the seam line (Figure B). Place the two HST units right sides together with opposite colors facing one another. Stitch ¼" on either side of the drawn line.

Figure B

4. Cut apart on the drawn line, leaving a ¼" seam allowance and making two QST units (Figure C).

Figure C

5. Open and press to complete two QST units, also known as hourglass units when made of two contrasting fabrics (Figure D). ●

Figure D

DESIGNED & QUILTED BY PREETI HARRIS

Stars & Swirls

Interlocking stars float across this swirling galaxy. An unexpected secondary design is formed where blocks intersect.

SKILL LEVEL
Confident Beginner

FINISHED SIZES
Quilt Size: 72" x 88"
Block Size: 8" x 8"
Number of Blocks: 99

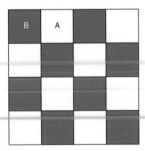

16-Patch
8" x 8" Finished Block
Make 20

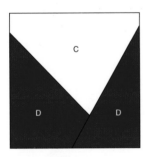

Star Point
8" x 8" Finished Block
Make 79

MATERIALS
- 6 yards white*
- 2¼ yards total of 3 to 4 assorted greens*
- 2¼ yards total of 3 to 4 assorted reds*
- 1¾ yards total of 3 to 4 assorted dark reds*
- 5 yards backing
- 80" x 96" batting
- Thread
- Basic sewing tools and supplies

Sunset Plains from Island Batik used to make sample. EQ8 was used to design this quilt.

PROJECT NOTES
Read all instructions before beginning this project.

Stitch right sides together using a ¼" seam allowance unless otherwise specified.

Materials and cutting lists assume 40" of usable fabric width.

Arrows indicate directions to press seams.

WOF – width of fabric
HST – half-square triangle
QST – quarter-square triangle

CUTTING
From white cut:
- 20 (8½" x WOF) strips, then subcut a total of 80 (8½") C squares
- 11 (2½" x WOF) A strips for strip sets
- 10 (2½" x WOF) binding strips

From assorted greens cut:
- 4 (2½" x WOF) B strips for strip sets
- 6 (8½" x WOF) strips, then subcut a total of 24 (8½") D squares. Cut each square once diagonally, keeping matching triangles together

From assorted reds cut:
- 4 (2½" x WOF) B strips for strip sets
- 7 (8½" x WOF) strips, then subcut a total of 28 (8½") D squares. Cut each square once diagonally, keeping matching triangles together

From assorted dark reds cut:
- 3 (2½" x WOF) B strips for strip sets
- 7 (8½" x WOF) strips, then subcut a total of 28 (8½") D squares. Cut each square once diagonally, keeping matching triangles together

Fabric Notes

For every 16-Patch block, make four Star Point blocks. One Star Point block will be left over. When arranging the blocks into star shapes for the quilt top, choose a different (not matching) color for the center of the star. For example, with green Star Point blocks, use either a red or dark red 16-Patch block at the center.

COMPLETING THE BLOCKS
16-Patch Blocks

1. Join an A and a B WOF strip along long sides (Figure 1). Press. Repeat with all remaining A and B strips to make 11 assorted A-B strip sets.

Figure 1

2. Cut each strip set in half and sew two matching half strip sets together along long sides, alternating fabrics, to make 11 A-B strip sets 8½" high x at least 20" long (Figure 2).

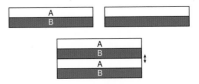

Figure 2

3. Cut each strip set into eight segments 2½" wide (Figure 3). Keep matching A-B segments together.

Figure 3

4. Referring to the 16-Patch block diagram for orientation, arrange four matching segments so fabrics alternate. Sew segments together to complete a 16-Patch block. Make 20 blocks (seven each red and green, and six dark red. There are extra segments to allow for variety if desired when making blocks).

Star Point Blocks

1. Use a removable fabric marker to draw a diagonal line from corner to corner on the right side of a C square (Figure 4). Cut 1½" away from the line and discard the trimmed-off corner triangle. You can also use a rotary cutting ruler, aligning the 1½" line with two opposite corners, and cut along the edge.

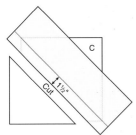

Figure 4

2. Place a D triangle along the trimmed edge of C as shown, then pin in place and sew (Figure 5). Press D triangle open, then trim D even with C sides to 8½" square.

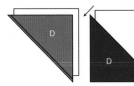

Figure 5

3. Referring to the Star Point block diagram and Figure 6, place the matching D triangle on the adjacent side of the C square as shown, sew, then press D open and trim again to 8½" square to complete a Star Point block. Trim the excess corner underneath the D triangle just added, leaving a ¼" seam allowance.

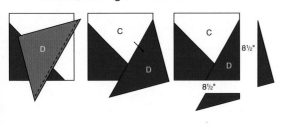

Figure 6

4. Repeat Steps 1–3 to make a total of 79 Star Point blocks, varying the angles of the points if desired. Keep blocks together in sets of four of the same star point fabrics.

COMPLETING THE QUILT

1. Referring to the Assembly Diagram for block placement and orientation, arrange blocks in 11 rows of nine blocks each.

2. Join blocks into rows, then join rows to complete the quilt top. Press.

3. Layer, baste, quilt as desired and bind referring to Quilting Basics. ●

Here Are Tips

Step away and look at the layout from about 10 feet. If all the Star Point blocks are correctly placed, the swirls created by the background fabric will appear.

Use the 16-Patch seams as a guide to quilt a 2" grid.

Stars & Swirls
Assembly Diagram 72" x 88"

DESIGN BY CHRIS MALONE

Winter Days Tote

The holidays are a busy time with lots of errands and visiting. This patchwork tote, with its serene snowy scene, can carry all the necessities. It also makes a thoughtful gift!

SKILL LEVEL
Beginner

FINISHED SIZE
Tote Size: 15" x 12" x 6"

MATERIALS
- ⅞ yard gray print
- ⅞ yard total assorted gray and white tonals and prints
- ⅛ yard red dot
- Small piece each brown, light red, gold and three green tonals, and black solid
- 22" x 35" piece batting*
- 1 (³⁄₁₆"-diameter) white button
- ⅜ yard 18"-wide fusible web with paper release
- Template material
- Thread*
- Basic sewing tools and supplies

Warm & Natural batting from The Warm Company; 100% Cotton Thread from Aurifil used to make sample.

PROJECT NOTES
Read all instructions before beginning this project.

Stitch right sides together using a ¼" seam allowance unless otherwise specified.

Materials and cutting lists assume 40" of usable fabric width.

Refer to photo and diagram for placement of appliqués.

CUTTING

From gray print cut:
- 2 (15½" x 21½") B rectangles
- 2 (3½" x 18") D strips
- 1 (6½") C square

From assorted gray and white tonals and prints cut:
- 74 (3½") A squares total

From red dot cut:
- 2 (2½" x 18") E strips

From batting cut:
- 2 (15½" x 21½") rectangles
- 2 (3½" x 18") strips

COMPLETING THE TOTE EXTERIOR

1. Arrange 35 A squares into five rows of seven squares each for the tote front. Repeat for the tote back. (Reserve remaining four squares for pocket.) Sew the squares together in each row. Sew the rows together to make the exterior tote pieces.

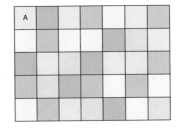

Figure 1

2. Place the pieced front, right side up, on a batting rectangle and baste all around, about ³⁄₁₆" from the edge. Repeat for the pieced back.

3. Prepare templates for the bird body, wing, beak and face patch; and leaf, branch and berry templates using the patterns provided. Trace the shapes onto the paper side of the fusible web in the quantities listed below. Cut the shapes apart and fuse to the wrong side of the appliqué fabrics as listed below. Cut out on pattern lines and remove paper backing.
- Red dot: 1 each bird body and wing
- Gold tonal: 1 beak
- Black solid: 1 face patch
- Brown tonal: 1 branch
- Green tonals: 3 leaves
- Light red: 5 berries

4. Center the branch about 7" down from the top edge of the tote front (Figure 2). Arrange the bird body overlapping the branch slightly with the wing at an angle as shown in the Placement Diagram. Place the face patch on the head with the beak overlapping the edge. Arrange one leaf in front of the bird and two leaves behind the bird with the berries arranged at the bases of the leaves. Fuse appliqués in place.

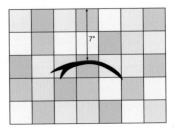

Figure 2

5. Machine blanket-stitch around all the appliqués using matching thread.

6. Quilt the tote front and back as desired. The photographed tote is quilted with straight lines about ¼" from the seams.

7. Sew the button to the bird for an eye.

8. Cut out a 3" x 3" square from the bottom corners of both pieced front and back rectangles (Figure 3).

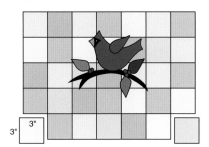

Figure 3

9. Pin the front and back together, right sides facing, and sew the side and bottom seams; press seams open (Figure 4).

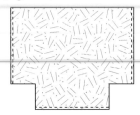

Figure 4

10. To shape the bottom of the bag, fold a bottom corner up so the side seam aligns with the bottom seam and stitch across (Figure 5). Repeat on the opposite corner. Turn bag right side out.

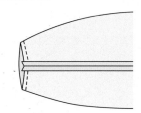

Figure 5

COMPLETING THE TOTE

1. To prepare the handles, layer a batting strip; gray D strip, right side up; and red dot E strip, right side down, with one long edge of the E strip even with the edges of the batting and D strip. Sew ¼" from edge (Figure 6). Trim batting close to seam. Make two.

Figure 6

2. Pull red E strip over so the second long edge is aligned with the batting and D strip and sew again (Figure 7). Trim batting close to seam. Make two.

Make 2

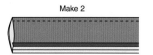

Figure 7

3. Turn strip right side out through one end. Press flat with the red E strip centered on the gray D strip. Topstitch by stitching in the ditch of the seam (Figure 8). Make two.

Make 2

Figure 8

4. Pin the end of one handle at the top of the tote front, about 4½" from the side seam and with right sides together (Figure 9). Pin the other end in the same manner, 4½" from the other side seam. Baste to secure. Repeat with the second handle on the tote back.

Figure 9

5. To make the interior pocket, arrange the remaining four A squares into two rows of two squares each (Figure 10). Sew the squares together in each row; sew the rows together to complete the pocket front.

Figure 10   **Figure 11**

6. Pin the pocket front and the C square together and sew all around, leaving an opening on one side for turning (Figure 11). Trim the corners and turn right side out. Press the edges flat. Fold in the seam allowance on the opening and press. Stitch across the top edge of the pocket.

7. Center and pin the pocket on one B rectangle, about 2¼" down from the top edge (Figure 12). Stitch the sides and bottom close to the edge, backstitching to secure the stitches.

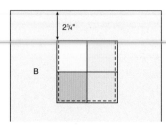

Figure 12

8. To make the lining, repeat steps 8–10 of Completing the Tote Exterior. Leave a 6" opening in the bottom seam and do not turn right side out.

9. Slip the tote exterior inside the lining, placing the tote exterior facing the right side of the lining and matching the side seams and the top edge. Stitch around the top edge.

10. Reach through the opening in the lining and pull the tote exterior out. Hand-stitch the opening closed and push the lining inside the tote. Press the top edges flat and topstitch all around the top edge to complete the tote. ●

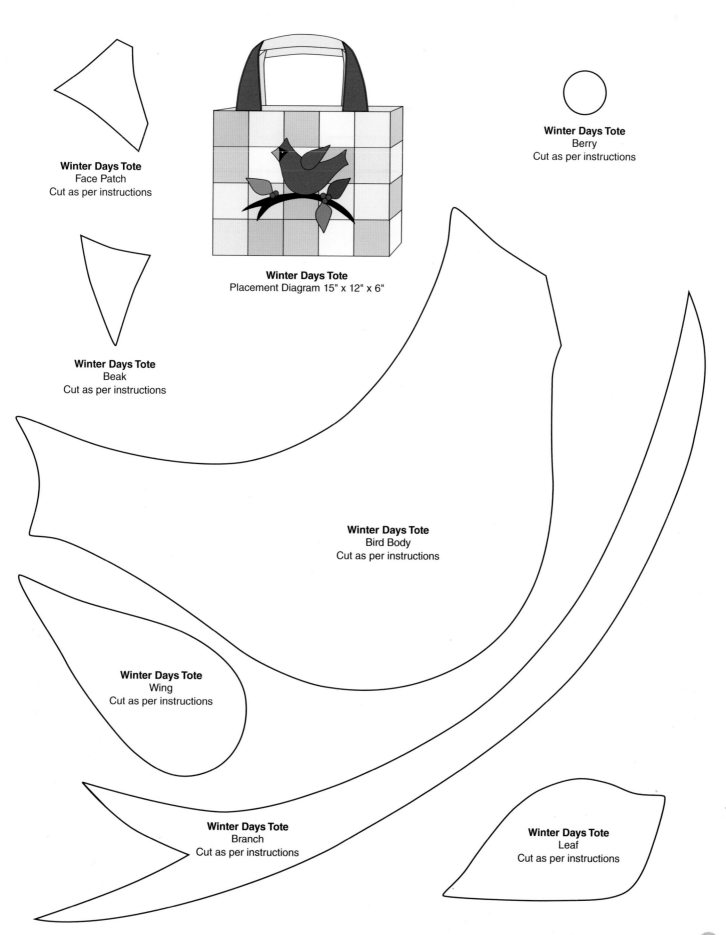

Winter Days Tote
Face Patch
Cut as per instructions

Winter Days Tote
Placement Diagram 15" x 12" x 6"

Winter Days Tote
Berry
Cut as per instructions

Winter Days Tote
Beak
Cut as per instructions

Winter Days Tote
Bird Body
Cut as per instructions

Winter Days Tote
Wing
Cut as per instructions

Winter Days Tote
Branch
Cut as per instructions

Winter Days Tote
Leaf
Cut as per instructions

DESIGNED & QUILTED BY JOY HEIMARK

Elegant Trails

Classic Snail's Trail blocks in vibrant Christmas hues combine to make a winding design that draws the eye to each swirl.

SKILL LEVEL
Intermediate

FINISHED SIZES
Quilt Size: 72" x 72"
Block Size: 8" x 8", 8" x 2"
Number of Blocks: 36, 84

Sashing
8" x 2" Finished Block
Make 84

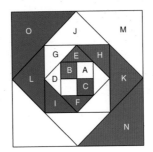

Snail's Trail
8" x 8" Finished Block
Make 36

PROJECT NOTES
Read all instructions before beginning this project.

Stitch right sides together using a ¼" seam allowance unless otherwise specified.

Materials and cutting lists assume 40" of usable fabric width.

WOF – width of fabric
HST – half-square triangle ☐
QST – quarter-square triangle ⊠

MATERIALS
- 2⅛ yards white*
- 2 yards gold*
- 1⅞ yards black*
- 1¾ yards dark green*
- 1⅝ yards red*
- 1⅛ yards green*
- 4⅝ yards backing
- 80" x 80" batting
- Thread
- Paper-piecing paper
- Basic sewing tools and supplies

Holiday at Home collection and Basics from Island Batik used to make sample.

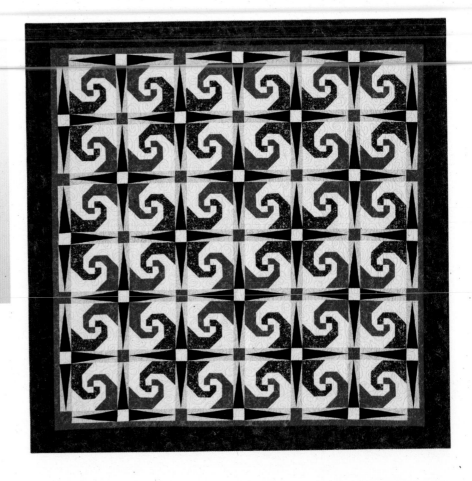

"Snail's Trail blocks have been on my quilting bucket list, and these Christmas fabrics helped me decide to finally make them. I mimicked the trails in my quilting and then echoed the sashing elements in the outer border quilting." —Joy Heimark

CUTTING

From white cut:

- 18 (5¼") J squares, then cut each twice diagonally ⊠ to yield 72 J triangles
- 36 (5") M squares; then cut each once diagonally ◺ to yield 72 M triangles
- 18 (3¼") D squares, then cut each twice diagonally ⊠ to yield 72 D triangles
- 36 (2⅞") G squares; then cut each once diagonally ◺ to yield 72 G triangles
- 24 (2½") R squares
- 4 (1½" x WOF) strips for A strip sets

From gold cut:

- 7 (10" x WOF) strips, then subcut into: 84 (10" x 3") Q rectangles

From black cut:

- 7 (9" x WOF) strips, then subcut into: 84 (9" x 3") P rectangles

From dark green cut:

- 8 (4½" x WOF) strips, stitch short ends to short ends, then subcut into: 2 (4½" x 64½") V and 2 (4½" x72½") W outer border strips
- 9 (2½" x WOF) binding strips

From red cut:

- 9 (5¼") K squares, then cut each twice diagonally ⊠ to yield 36 K triangles
- 18 (5") N squares; then cut each once diagonally ◺ to yield 36 N triangles
- 9 (3¼") E squares, then cut each twice diagonally ⊠ to yield 36 E triangles
- 18 (2⅞") H squares, then cut each once diagonally ◺ to yield 36 H triangles
- 25 (2½") S squares

- 6 (1½" x WOF) strips, stitch short ends to short ends, then subcut into: 2 (1½" x 62½") T and 2 (1½" x 64½") U inner border strips
- 2 (1½" x WOF) strips for B strip sets

From green cut:

- 9 (5¼") L squares, then cut each twice diagonally ⊠ to yield 36 L triangles
- 18 (5") O squares, then cut each once diagonally ◺ to yield 36 O triangles
- 9 (3¼") F squares, then cut each twice diagonally ⊠ to yield 36 F triangles
- 18 (2⅞") I squares, then cut each once diagonally ◺ to yield 36 I triangles
- 2 (1½" x WOF) strips for C strip sets

COMPLETING THE BLOCKS

Snail's Trail Blocks

1. Join an A and a B strip along long edges to make an A-B strip set (Figure 1). Make two. Cut 36 1½"-wide A-B segments. Repeat with A and C strips to make two A-C strip sets and cut 36 1½"-wide A-C segments.

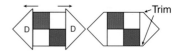

Figure 1

2. Join an A-B and an A-C segment as shown to make a four-patch unit (Figure 2). Make 36.

Four-Patch Unit
Make 36

Figure 2

3. Sew D triangles, centered, to opposite sides of a four-patch unit, noting B and C orientation (Figure 3). Press. If desired, trim tips of D triangles even with the raw edges of the four-patch.

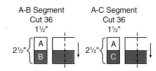

Figure 3

4. Sew an E triangle, centered, to the B side of a four-patch unit, then add an F triangle to the opposite side to complete round 1 of the block (Figure 4). Press. Trim the unit to square up to 3⅜", making sure to trim ¼" from seam intersections so as not to lose the triangle points.

Figure 4

5. Referring to the Snail's Trail block diagram, continue adding G–O triangles in alphabetical order in the same manner. Trim as needed as follows: after adding the I triangle, square up to 4½", then after adding the L triangle, square up to 6⅛". Square up the finished block if needed to 8½". Make 36.

Sashing Units

1. Make 84 copies of the sashing unit foundation pattern.

2. Mark 42 Q rectangles, oriented vertically as shown, ½" in from the top left and bottom right corners (Figure 5). Cut diagonally from mark to mark to yield 84 Q triangles. Repeat to mark and cut the remaining Q rectangles in the opposite direction as shown to yield 84 Q reversed triangles.

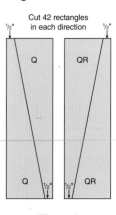

Figure 5

3. Referring to Paper Piecing and the Sashing block diagram, paper-piece each sashing unit using the Q and Q reversed triangles and P rectangles. Since these units are large, if desired remove the paper after trimming, rather than waiting until after quilt top is assembled.

COMPLETING THE QUILT

1. Referring to the Assembly Diagram, lay out the blocks in six rows of six blocks each, noting the placement of the blocks. Add sashing units between each block and at the beginning and end of each row, rotating every other sashing unit as shown. Lay out the remaining sashing units, oriented as shown, and R and S cornerstones in seven sashing rows with six sashing units and seven cornerstones in each row.

2. Sew block row pieces together, pressing toward blocks. Sew sashing row pieces together, pressing toward R/S.

3. Join block and sashing rows together to complete the quilt center. Remove foundation papers now if not previously removed. Press.

4. Sew T–W border strips to the quilt center in alphabetical order, starting with the left/right sides, then the top and bottom. Press toward the borders.

5. Layer, baste, quilt as desired and bind referring to Quilting Basics. ●

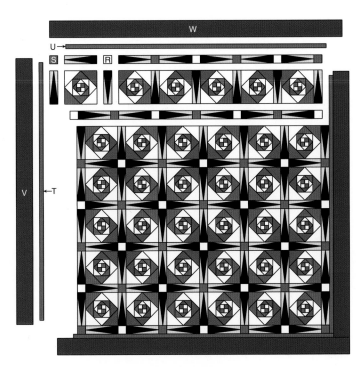

Elegant Trails
Assembly Diagram 72" x 72"

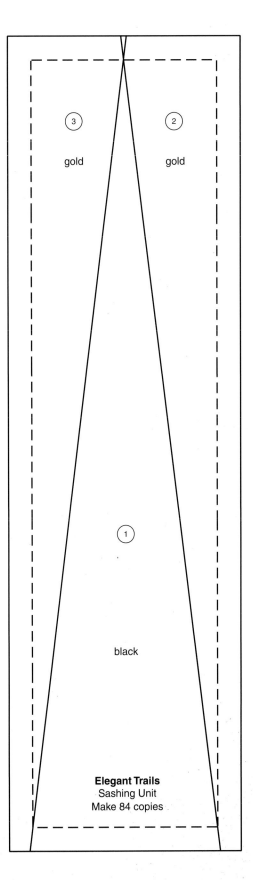

③ gold

② gold

① black

Elegant Trails
Sashing Unit
Make 84 copies

PAPER PIECING

Paper piecing allows a quilter to make blocks with odd-shaped and/or small pieces and more precise corners. Fabric pieces are sewn together onto the reverse side of a paper-piecing pattern, and then the paper is carefully removed when the block is completed. You may have to rethink how you piece when using this technique, and it does require a little more yardage.

1. Make same-size copies of the paper-piecing pattern as directed in the pattern. There are several choices in transparent papers as well as water-soluble papers that can be used, which are available at your local office supply store, quilt shop or online. Some papers can be used in your printer.

2. Cut out the patterns, leaving a margin around the outside bold lines as shown in Figure A. All patterns are reversed on the paper copies. Pattern color choices can be written in each numbered space on the marked side of each copy.

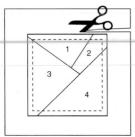

Figure A

3. When cutting fabric for paper piecing, the pieces do not have to be the exact size and shape of the area to be covered. Cut fabric pieces the general shape and ¼"–½" larger than the design area to be covered. This makes paper piecing a good way to use up scraps.

4. With the printed side of the pattern facing you, fold along each line of the pattern as shown in Figure B, creasing the stitching lines. This will help in trimming the fabric seam allowances and in removing the paper

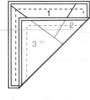

Figure B

when you are finished stitching. **Note:** *You can also machine-stitch along the lines with a basting stitch and no thread to perforate the paper.*

5. Turn the paper pattern over with the unmarked side facing you and position fabric indicated on pattern right side up over the space marked 1. Hold the paper up to a window or over a light box to make sure that the fabric overlaps all sides of space 1 at least ¼" as shown in Figure C from the printed side of the pattern. Pin to hold fabric in place. **Note:** *You can also use a light touch of glue stick. Too much glue will make the paper difficult to remove.*

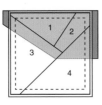 

Figure C   **Figure D**

6. Turn the paper over with the right side of the paper facing you, and fold the paper along the lines between sections 1 and 2. Trim fabric to about ¼" from the folded edge as shown in Figure D.

7. Place the second fabric indicated right sides together with first piece. Fabric edges should be even along line between spaces 1 and 2 as shown in Figure E. Fold fabric over and check to see if second fabric piece will cover space 2.

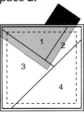

Figure E   **Figure F**

8. With the right side of the paper facing you, hold fabric pieces together and stitch along the line between spaces 1 and 2 as shown in Figure F using a very small stitch length (18–20 stitches per inch). **Note:** *Using a smaller stitch length*

will make removing paper easier because it creates a tear line at the seam. Always begin and end seam by sewing two to three stitches beyond the line. You do not need to backstitch. Start sewing at the solid outside line of the pattern when the beginning of the seam is at the edge of the pattern.

9. Turn the pattern over, flip the second fabric back and finger-press as shown in Figure G.

 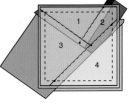

Figure G   **Figure H**

10. Continue trimming and sewing pieces in numerical order until the pattern is completely covered. Make sure pieces along the outer edge extend past the solid line to allow for a ¼" seam allowance as shown in Figure H.

11. When the whole block is sewn, press the block and trim all excess fabric from the block along the outside-edge solid line of the paper pattern as shown in Figure I.

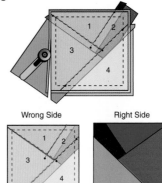

Figure I

12. After stitching blocks together, carefully remove the backing paper from completed blocks and press seams. You can also staystitch ⅛" from the outer edge of the completed block. Carefully remove backing paper and press seams. Then complete quilt top assembly. ●

DESIGNS BY CHRIS MALONE

Making Spirits Bright

Whether you are bringing a bottle of wine to a get-together or giving one for a gift, these bags will garner attention. They are appliquéd, quilted, fully lined and reusable, but they are so simple to make.

MATERIALS

- 4 (7" x 16") batting rectangles
- Fusible web with paper release
- Template material
- Thread
- Basic sewing tools and supplies

For Santa Bag:

- ¼ yard or fat quarter green holly print
- ¼ yard or fat quarter white holly print
- Small piece each red dot, white dot, white tonal and pink solid
- ³⁄₁₆"-diameter buttons: 2 black, and 1 each pink and white
- 1 (⅞"-diameter) red button
- 1 yard (⅞"-wide) red ribbon

For Gnome Tote:

- ¼ yard or fat quarter gray swirl print
- ¼ yard or fat quarter green/white print
- Small piece each green dot, white/gray print, pink solid, dark gray tonal and dark red tonal
- 1 (½"-diameter) white button

SKILL LEVEL
Beginner

FINISHED SIZE
Bag Size: 3½" x 16" x 3"

PROJECT NOTES
Read all instructions before beginning this project.

Stitch right sides together using a ¼" seam allowance unless otherwise specified.

Materials and cutting lists assume 40" of usable fabric width for yardage and 20" for fat quarters.

Arrows indicate directions to press seams.

WOF – width of fabric

HST – half-square triangle

QST – quarter-square triangle

CUTTING
From green holly print cut:
- 2 (7" x 16") A rectangles

From white holly print cut:
- 2 (7" x 16") B rectangles

From gray swirl print cut:
- 2 (7" x 16") C rectangles
- 2 (3" x 9") E strips

From green/white print cut:
- 2 (7" x 16") D rectangles

COMPLETING THE BAGS
Santa Bag

1. Referring to Raw-Edge Fusible Appliqué on page 47, prepare templates for Santa hat, hat trim, face, beard and mustache half using patterns provided. Then make the following appliqués:

- Red dot: 1 Santa hat
- White dot: 1 hat trim
- Pink solid: 1 face
- White tonal: 1 beard; 2 mustache halves, reversing pattern for 1

2. Refer to the photograph while constructing the Santa. Center the beard 3" up from the bottom of one A rectangle. Add the face above the beard and the hat above the face.

3. Place the hat trim overlapping the face and hat. Add the mustache halves at the top of the beard as shown. Fuse appliqués in place.

4. Baste a batting rectangle to the wrong side of each A rectangle (Figure 1).

Figure 1

5. Machine blanket-stitch around the edges of the appliqués using matching thread. (Finishing the edges with the batting in place simultaneously "quilts" the appliqué design.) Add other quilting to both pieces if desired.

6. Sew the two black buttons to the face for eyes and the pink button in the center for a nose. Sew the white button to the tip of the hat.

7. Pin the bag front and back of the bag together, right sides facing (Figure 2), and sew the long sides and across the bottom edge (Figure 3).

Figure 2   **Figure 3**

8. To make a box bottom for the bag, fold the bottom seam up to match the seam on the side. Lay bag with bottom facing up. Measure and mark a line 1½" in from the point (Figure 4).

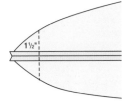

Figure 4

9. Make sure the bag underneath the marked corner is spread out flat to avoid puckering. Sew on the line, backstitching at each end. Trim the seam to ¼". Repeat on the other side to complete the box bottom. Turn bag right side out.

10. Repeat steps 7–9 using the B rectangles. Leave a 4" opening on one long side. Do not turn right side out (Figure 5).

Figure 5

11. Slip the bag exterior inside the lining, matching side seams. Right sides will be together. Sew all around the top edge. (Figure 6).

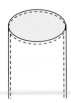

Figure 6

12. To turn right side out, reach into the opening on the lining and pull the bag and lining through. Fold in the seam allowance on the opening in the liner and stitch closed by hand or machine. Push the lining into the bag and press the top edge. Topstitch ¼" from the top (Figure 7).

Figure 7

13. Measure 15" from one end of the ribbon and mark with a pin. Measure down 3" from the top of the bag in the center back and place the marked ribbon at this point. Hold the red button over the ribbon and sew through the button, ribbon and bag back to attach (Figure 8).

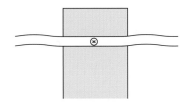

Figure 8

14. Insert wine bottle into bag and wrap longer ribbon length around front of bag then tie in a bow on the side. Trim ribbon ends as needed.

Gnome Tote

1. Referring to Raw-Edge Fusible Appliqué, prepare templates for gnome robe, arm #1 and #2, hat, beard, mustache half, nose, hand, boot and wine glass using patterns provided to make the following appliqués:

- Green dot: 1 each gnome robe, arm #1, arm #2 and hat
- White/gray print: 1 beard; 2 mustache halves, reversing pattern for 1
- Pink solid: 1 each nose and hand
- Dark gray tonal: 2 boots
- Dark red tonal: 1 wine glass

2. Refer to the photograph while constructing the Gnome. Center the gnome robe 3" up from the bottom of one C rectangle. Slip arm #1 under the left side of the robe and arm #2 at the other side with the hand overlapping the edge.

3. Place the hat above the robe then put the beard on, overlapping the hat and robe. Add the mustache halves and nose.

4. Place the boots at the center bottom and the wine glass just above the top of the hand as shown. Fuse appliqués in place.

5. Baste a batting rectangle to the wrong side of each C rectangle.

6. Machine blanket-stitch around the edges of the appliqués using matching thread. (Finishing the edges with the batting in place simultaneously "quilts" the appliqué design.)

7. Add other quilting to the bag front and back as desired. To complete the wine glass, transfer the pattern and stitch with black thread. Stitch a second time over the lines to make them bolder.

8. Sew the white button to the top of the hat.

9. Follow steps 7–9 of the Santa Bag instructions to make the outside of the tote with a box bottom.

10. To make the handles, fold an E strip in half lengthwise, wrong sides facing, and press. Open strip and fold each long side in almost to the crease and press (Figure 9a). Refold the strip in half, press and topstitch

close to the edge on both long sides (Figure 9b). Repeat to make a second handle.

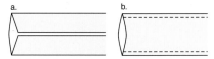

Figure 9

11. Pin one end of a handle 1½" from the right-side seam of the tote front with raw edges even with the top of the bag. Pin the other end 1½" from the left-side seam (Figure 10). Baste in place and repeat with the remaining handle on the tote back.

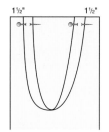

Figure 10

12. Follow steps 10–12 of the Santa Bag instructions to complete the tote, using the D rectangles for the lining. ●

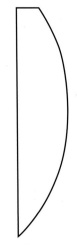

Making Spirits Bright
Gnome Arm #1
Cut as per instructions

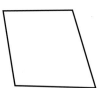

Making Spirits Bright
Gnome Arm #2
Cut as per instructions

Making Spirits Bright
Gnome Boot
Cut as per instructions

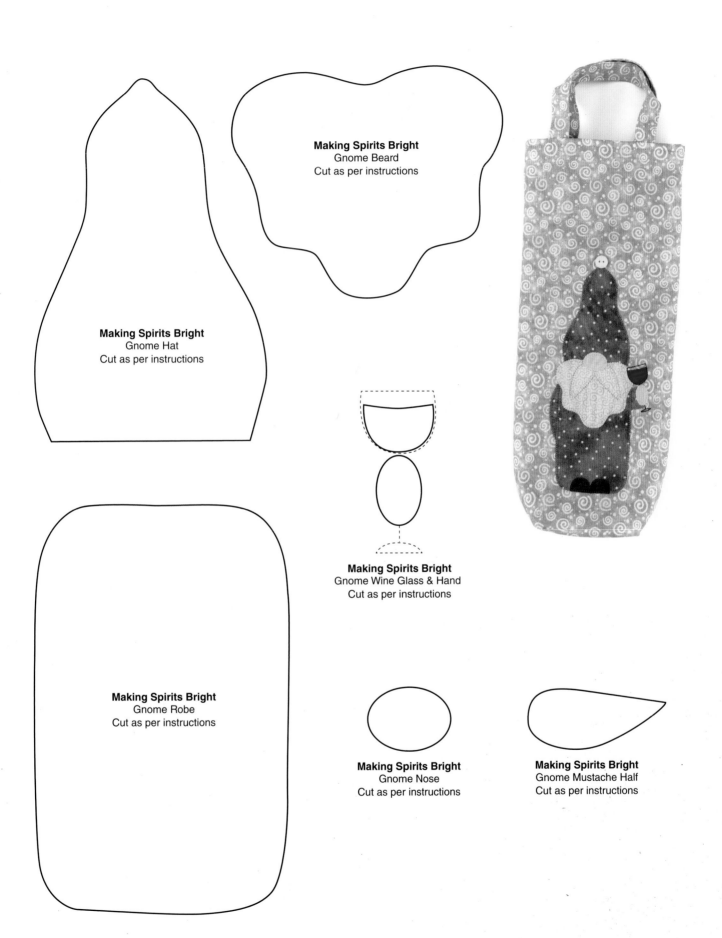

Making Spirits Bright
Gnome Hat
Cut as per instructions

Making Spirits Bright
Gnome Beard
Cut as per instructions

Making Spirits Bright
Gnome Wine Glass & Hand
Cut as per instructions

Making Spirits Bright
Gnome Robe
Cut as per instructions

Making Spirits Bright
Gnome Nose
Cut as per instructions

Making Spirits Bright
Gnome Mustache Half
Cut as per instructions

Making Spirits Bright
Santa Face
Cut as per instructions

Making Spirits Bright
Santa Hat Trim
Cut as per instructions

Making Spirits Bright
Santa Mustache Half
Cut as per instructions

Making Spirits Bright
Santa Beard
Cut as per instructions

Making Spirits Bright
Santa Hat
Cut as per instructions

RAW-EDGE FUSIBLE APPLIQUÉ

One of the easiest ways to appliqué is the raw-edge fusible-web method. Individual pieces of paper-backed fusible web are fused to the wrong side of specified fabrics, cut out and then fused together in a motif or individually to a foundation fabric, where they are machine-stitched in place.

Choosing Appliqué Fabrics

Depending on the appliqué, you may want to consider using batiks. Batik is a much tighter weave and, because of the manufacturing process, does not fray. If you are thinking about using regular quilting cottons, be sure to stitch your raw-edge appliqués with blanket/buttonhole stitches instead of a straight stitch.

Cutting Appliqué Pieces

1. Fusible appliqué shapes should be reversed for this technique.

2. Trace the appliqué shapes onto the paper side of paper-backed fusible web. Leave at least ¼" between shapes. Cut out shapes leaving a margin around traced lines. **Note:** *If doing several identical appliqués, trace reversed shapes onto template material to make reusable templates for tracing shapes onto the fusible web.*

3. Follow manufacturer's instructions and fuse shapes to wrong side of fabric as indicated on pattern for color and number to cut.

4. Cut out appliqué shapes on traced lines. Remove paper backing from shapes.

5. Again following fusible web manufacturer's instructions, arrange and fuse pieces to quilt referring to quilt pattern. Or fuse together shapes on top of an appliqué ironing mat to make an appliqué motif that can then be fused to the quilt.

Stitching Appliqué Edges

Machine-stitch appliqué edges to secure the appliqués in place and help finish the raw edges with matching or invisible thread (Photo A). **Note:** *To show stitching, all samples have been stitched with contrasting thread.*

Photo A

Invisible thread can be used to stitch appliqués down when using the blanket or straight stitches. Do not use it for the satin stitch. Definitely practice with invisible thread before using it on your quilt; it can sometimes be difficult to work with.

A short, narrow buttonhole or blanket stitch is most commonly used (Photo B). Your machine manual may also refer to this as an appliqué stitch. Be sure to stitch next to the appliqué edge with the stitch catching the appliqué.

 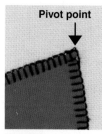

Photo B   **Photo C**

Practice turning inside and outside corners on scrap fabric before stitching appliqué pieces. Learn how your machine stitches so that you can make the pivot points smooth (Photo C).

1. To stitch outer corners, stitch to the edge of the corner and stop with needle in the fabric at the corner point. Pivot to the next side of the corner and continue to sew (Photo D). You will get a box on an outside corner.

Photo D

2. To stitch inner corners, pivot at the inner point with needle in fabric (Photo E). You will see a Y shape in the corner.

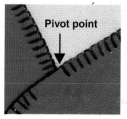

Photo E

3. You can also use a machine straight stitch. Turn corners in the same manner, stitching to the corners and pivoting with needle in down position (Photos F and G).

Photo F   **Photo G**

General Appliqué Tips

1. Use a light- to medium-weight stabilizer behind an appliqué to keep the fabric from puckering during machine stitching (Photo H).

Photo H

2. To reduce the stiffness of a finished appliqué, cut out the center of the fusible web shape, leaving ¼"–½" inside the pattern line. This gives a border of adhesive to fuse to the background and leaves the center soft and easy to quilt.

3. If an appliqué fabric is so light colored or thin that the background fabric shows through, fuse a lightweight interfacing to the wrong side of the fabric. You can also fuse a piece of the appliqué fabric to a matching piece, wrong sides together, and then apply the fusible web with a drawn pattern to one side. ●

Quilting Basics

The following is a reference guide. For more information, consult a comprehensive quilting book.

Quilt Backing & Batting

Cut your backing and batting 8" larger than the finished quilt-top size and 4" larger for quilts smaller than 50" square. **Note:** *Check with longarm quilter about their requirements, if applicable. For baby quilts not going to a longarm quilter 4"–6" overall may be sufficient.* If preparing the backing from standard-width fabrics, remove the selvages and sew two or three lengths together; press seams open. If using 108"-wide fabric, trim to size on the straight grain of the fabric. Prepare batting the same size as your backing.

Quilting

1. Press quilt top on both sides and trim all loose threads. **Note:** *If you are sending your quilt to a longarm quilter, contact them for specifics about preparing your quilt for quilting.*

2. Mark quilting design on quilt top. Make a quilt sandwich by layering the backing right side down, batting and quilt top centered right side up on flat surface and smooth out. Baste layers together using pins, thread basting or spray basting to hold. **Note:** *Tape or pin backing to surface to hold taut while layering and avoid puckers.*

3. Quilt as desired by hand or machine. Remove pins or basting as you quilt.

4. Trim batting and backing edges even with raw edges of quilt top.

Binding the Quilt

1. Join binding strips on short ends with diagonal seams to make one long strip; trim seams to ¼" and press seams open (Figure 1).

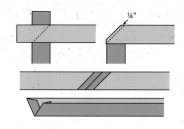

Figure 1

2. Fold ½" of one short end to wrong side and press. Fold the binding strip in half with wrong sides together along length, again referring to Figure 1; press.

3. Starting about 3" from the folded short end, sew binding to quilt top edges, matching raw edges and using a ¼" seam. Stop stitching ¼" from corner and backstitch (Figure 2).

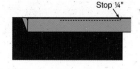

Stop ¼"

Figure 2

4. Fold binding up at a 45-degree angle to seam and then down even with quilt edges, forming a pleat at corner (Figure 3).

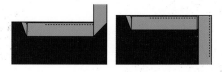

Figure 3

5. Resume stitching from corner edge as shown in Figure 3, down quilt side, backstitching ¼" from next corner. Repeat, mitering all corners, stitching to within 3" of starting point.

6. Trim binding, leaving enough length to tuck inside starting end and complete stitching (Figure 4).

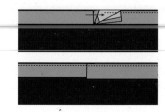

Figure 4

7. If stitching binding by hand, machine-sew binding to the front of the quilt and fold to the back before stitching. If stitching by machine, machine-sew binding to back of the quilt and fold to the front before stitching.

Published by Annie's, 306 East Parr Road, Berne, IN 46711. Printed in USA. Copyright © 2022 Annie's. All rights reserved. This publication may not be reproduced in part or in whole without written permission from the publisher.

RETAIL STORES: If you would like to carry this publication or any other Annie's publications, visit AnniesWSL.com.

Every effort has been made to ensure that the instructions in this publication are complete and accurate. We cannot, however, take responsibility for human error, typographical mistakes or variations in individual work. Please visit AnniesCustomerService.com to check for pattern updates.

ISBN: 978-1-64025-595-1

1 2 3 4 5 6 7 8 9